Initiat

INITIATION TO THE VEDAS

An abridged edition of
The Vedic Experience - Mantramañjarī

By

RAIMON PANIKKAR

Edited by

MILENA CARRARA PAVAN

MOTILAL BANARSIDASS PUBLISHERS
PRIVATE LIMITED • DELHI

First Edition: Delhi, 2006

ISBN: 81-208-2954-9

MOTILAL BANARSIDASS

41 U.A. Bungalow Road, Jawahar Nagar, Delhi 110 007
8 Mahalaxmi Chamber, 22 Bhulabhai Desai Road, Mumbai 400 026
120 Royapettah High Road, Mylapore, Chennai 600 004
236, 9th Main III Block, Jayanagar, Bangalore 560 011
Sanas Plaza, 1302 Baji Rao Road, Pune 411 002
8 Camac Street, Kolkata 700 017
Ashok Rajpath, Patna 800 004
Chowk, Varanasi 221 001

(explanation of the drawings):
On the cover and inside the book details of the same maṇḍala *(Samavasaraṇa-paṭṭa*
Rajastan, 1800) reproduced in crescendo to indicate the expansion of consciousness in
Man reaching the vision of Reality.

Printed in India
BY JAINENDRA PRAKASH JAIN AT SHRI JAINENDRA PRESS,
A-45 NARAINA, PHASE-I, NEW DELHI 110 028
AND PUBLISHED BY NARENDRA PRAKASH JAIN FOR
MOTILAL BANARSIDASS PUBLISHERS PRIVATE LIMITED,
BUNGALOW ROAD, DELHI 110 007

CONTENTS

PREFACE   7

THE VEDAS   11

ABBREVIATIONS   15

MANTRAMAÑJARĪ   17
    Agni
    Gāyatrī

I   DAWN AND BIRTH   25
    HYMN TO PRELUDE, *ādi*
    HYMN TO DAWN, *Uṣas*
    HYMN TO BIRTH, *prathamaṃ janma*

II GERMINATION AND GROWTH   35
    THE BREATH OF LIFE, *prāṇa*
    PRAYER FOR HAPPINESS, *svastyayana*

III. BLOSSOMING AND FULLNESS   45
    THE INNER LIGHT, *ātmajyotis*
    THE FIRE SACRIFICE, *agnihotra*
    SACRIFICE IS MAN, *puruṣayajña*

THE SACRIFICE OF THE MIND, *mānasayajña*
THE INTEGRAL ACTION, *karmayoga*

IV. FALL AND DECAY   55
    BEYOND SUFFER AND SUFFERING, *vītaśoka*
    PURIFYING KNOWLEDGE, *jñānāśuddhi*
    THE FIRE OF WISDOM, *jñānāgni*

V. DEATH AND DISSOLUTION   61
    THE GREAT DEPARTURE, *mahāprasthāna*
    WITHIN DEATH THERE IS IMMORTALITY,
    antaraṃ mṛtyor amṛtam

VI. NEW LIFE AND FREEDOM   69
    THE ASCENDING WAY, *brahmajāna*
    THE INTERNAL WAY, *puruṣo 'ntarātma*
    THE ENCOUNTER, *yoga*

VII. TWILIGHT   89
    PRAYERS AT SUNRISE
    PRAYERS AT SUNSET

LAST MANTRA   101
    LAST MANTRA

PREFACE

This short book is just an invitation to read *The Vedic Experience - Mantramañjarī* - An Anthology of the Vedas for Modern Man and Contemporary Celebration by Raimon Panikkar.

Such a book may not be easy reading, especially for those who are not familiar with indic culture, which has so much to offer provided that we approach it prodded not by mere curiosity, but urged by a genuine longing to discover in ourselves the morning light of humanity's primordial spiritual awareness.

"Initiation to the Vedas" is the title of this invitation to reanact the vedic experience, the human experience discovering the meaning of life in Man and in the World.

The title, however, could just as well be "Initiation of the Vedas" inasmuch as the book describes the path of initiation travelled by vedic Man becoming aware of Life in himself. Or, the title could even be "Initiation into the Vedas" since the entire body of the vedic hymns is nothing but a celebration of the rebirth of Man to the divine Life. The myths and rites constitute a symbolic universe through which Man touches the sacred, and thereby embraces reality.

Initiation, the existential experience necessary to reach the fullness of the human condition, represents one of the most significant events in human growth:

the ontological trasformation of Man, and consequently, the establishment of a new relation with life and the cosmos. Initiation is common to all ancient cultures and most world religions, but has been almost completely neglected in our modern society, even if it survives in the mystery of some rituals. Through initiation the sages hand down their teachings to new generations, transmitting the sense of the sacred, and the meaning of life and the cosmos.

May such teachings, which come from so far in time, find a rich soil in those of us who are willing to receive and set them in the colorful bouquet of the human experience. Such is the hope of Raimon Panikkar who has dedicated ten years of his life to translate the Vedas from sanskrit and to disclose their meaning through his commentaries. Through his numerous books the author tries to show the contemporary Man the way towards the ultimate experience. By discovering in himself the three dimensions of reality: the divine, the human and the cosmic, Man can reach his fullness and happiness.

"It is neither a question to go forward, searching for solutions, more powerful devices or simply more money, nor to go backward, as some conservatives would like, but to go beyond, that is, to re-discover the third dimension in ourselves enquiring again about the meaning of life, of reality and our role in it."

The aim of every culture, tradition and religion is the full happiness of Man. In order to recover the whole reality, a task that has become imperative today, we must allow our understanding of life to be enriched by that of others. This is why Panikkar attaches such importance to a cross-cultural approach to life, and has offered us this extraordinary contribution to that end.

Milano, 2005
Milena Carrara

THE VEDA

One of the most stupendous manifestations of the Spirit is undoubtedly that which has been handed down to us under the generic name of the *Vedas*. The word *Vedas*, which in sanskrit means knowledge, refers to the entire body of vedic literature appeared in the north of the indian peninsula about, or soon after, 2000 B.C. It was the result of an extraordinary intercultural encounter between the invading aryans, speaking an indo-european language, and the indigenous population who spoke a pre-dravidian language.

The *Veda* which include the four collections: *Atharva-veda, Yajur-veda* and *Ṛg-veda, Sāma-veda*, besides *Upaniṣads* and *Bhagavad-gītā* - were first chanted and recited, then written in the old indo-āryan language known as vedic, an ancestral language prior to the literary sanskrit.

This anthology is not a book on indian philosophy or even on hindū spirituality, and much less it is a typical work of indology; it is not an attempt to scrutinize the past for its own sake. It is rather an account of the vedic revelation, understood as an unveiling of depths that still resound in the heart of modern Man, so that he may become more conscious of his own human heritage and thus of the springs of his personal being. It aims, therefore, at presenting the *Vedas* as a human experience that is still valid and capable of enriching and challenging modern Man to live a fully human life, a life which does not just limit itself to actions and to a bi-dimentional space-time sphere, but that can reach its fullness through the complete realisation of any possibility.

The vedic experience unfolds the process of Man's "becoming conscious", of himself along with the three worlds and their mutual relationships. It is not the message of another party but the progressive enlightenment of reality itself.

This book amounts to an initiation path which, following the rythm of life in the cosmos, takes us to the realization of the birth of real Life in ourselves.

The hymns we find here are prayers. The whole universe vibrates at the sound of an authentic prayer: it is a "sacred action" if acted by the whole of our being as it embodies the whole reality.

To be able to invocate, that is, to call upon, something greater than ourselves, and so break our own boundaries, is the beginning of wisdom, the source of hope and the condition of joy.

The anthology consists of seven parts, which proceed according to a cosmic scheme following the disclosure of reality to human conscience. Two types of hymns have been chosen to illustrate each part: one concerning the cosmos and the other the Man.

I. *Dawn and Birth.* Preparation for emergence into existence, the tilling of the ground, or pre-existence and bursting into Being, into life.

II. *Germination and Growth*. The beginning, the striving, the affirmation of identity, the settling down in the realm of existence.

III. *Blossoming and Fullness*. The acme, the reaching of plenitude, of maturity, the zenith.

IV. *Fall and Decay*. The beginning of the downward path, the discovery that nothing resists the acids of time and that nobody is immune from the corrosion of existence.

V. *Death and Dissolution*. The destiny of all existing things, and the price that must be paid for having been alive and for having been a bearer of existence in time and space.

VI. *New Life and Freedom*. The marvelous mystery of Being, the re-emergence of life out of the ordeal of death, the disclosure that life is immortal, that Being is unfathomable, and that bliss and reality are capable of self-renewal.

VII. *Twilight*. The last part is like a ribbon that ties a bouquet. It is a collection of prayers to recite at sunrise and sunset, the celebration of the fullness of Life.

ABBREVIATIONS

AU	*Aitareya-upaniṣad*
AV	*Atharva-veda*
BG	*Bhagavad-gītā*
BU	*Bṛhadāraṇyaka-upaniṣad*
CU	*Chāndogya-upaniṣad*
IsU	*Īśa-upaniṣad*
KaivU	*Kaivalya-upaniṣad*
KathU	*Kaṭha-upaniṣad*
KausB	*Kauṣītaki-brāhmaṇa*
MahanarU	*Mahānārāyaṇa-upaniṣad*
MaitU	*Maitrī-upaniṣad*
MundU	*Muṇḍaka-upaniṣad*
PrasnU	*Praśna-upaniṣad*
RV	*Ṛg-veda*
SB	*Śatapatha-brāhmaṇa*
SuryU	*Sūrya-upaniṣad*
SU	*Śvetāśvatara-upaniṣad*
TU	*Taittirīya-upaniṣad*
U	*Upaniṣad*
V	*Veda*
YV	*Yajur-veda.*

MANTRAMAÑJARĪ

The subtitle of this anthology is *mantramañjarī,* which means *bouquet* of mantras.

Let's get ready to welcome this gift as if it were a bunch of flowers that the author offers us with the prayer of admiring them for their beauty with pure heart, without prejudices, as we should watch the lilies of the field which the *Gospels* talk about, so that we can be penetrated by their beauty.

Mantra stands for a sacred word, a sacrificial formula, an efficient counsel of a guru; it is neither a mere sound nor a sheer spell. Living words have a power that trascends the simple mental plane. To perceive the energy of the word one has to grasp not only its meaning but also its message, or its vibrations, as they are sometimes called to stress the link with the sound itself.

Faith, understanding, and physical utterance are essential requisites for an authentic mantra. Every word links us up with the source of all words. The ultimate character of the word, *vāc,* is a fundamental concept in indian spirituality.

Agni

The opening mantra is an invocation to Agni, the mediator par excellence, the sacrificial Fire, who transforms all material and human gifts into spiritual and divine realities, so that they may reach their endless destination. Agni has a priestly role and a threefold composition, his nature being theanthropocosmic (divine, human and earthly at one and the same time). This verse contains as in a nutshell the whole of Man's primordial religiousness: praise, mediation, sacrifice, commerce with the divine, all caught up in an atmosphere of invocation. We invoke the divine - wherever it may be and however we may conceive it - because, filled with love, we sense within ourselves the need to open the sluices that enclose our finitude.

Om agnim īḷe purohitaṃ
yajñasya devam ṛtvijam
hotāraṃ ratnadhātamam

I magnify God, the Divine Fire,
the Priest, Minister of the sacrifice
the Offerer of oblation, supreme Giver of treasure
RV I, 1, 1

Gāyatrī

Then comes the most renowned mantra of the *Veda*, the *Gāyatrī*: it is addressed to the divine life-giver as supreme, symbolized in Savitṛ, the Sun. It is recited daily at sunrise and at sunset, usually at the ritual bath.

The *Gāyatrī* is a complete symbol of light. It is certainly much more than the epiphany of light; it is the light itself when the recitation is a real prayer, an assimilation to and an identification with that which is prayed. Each line emphasizes one aspect of light: the glorious splendor of the Ultimate, its own internal radiance, that is, the uncreatedness of light; the creating light, the communicative brightness of the uncreated Sun, Savitṛ, the brilliance of the living God who illumines everything; and, finally, the incidence of this divine light in our beings, and especially in our minds, making us refulgent ourselves and trasmitters of the same refulgence and converting us into light: light from light, splendor from splendor, oneness with the source of light, not in a ponderous ontological identity but in a "lightsome" identity of luminosity, totally transparent: *ātman-brahman.*

tat savitur vareṇyaṃ
bhargo devasya dhīmahi

dhiyo yo naḥ pracodayāt
Om
We meditate upon the glorious splendor
Of the vivifier divine.
May he himself illuminate our minds!
Om
RV III, 62, 10

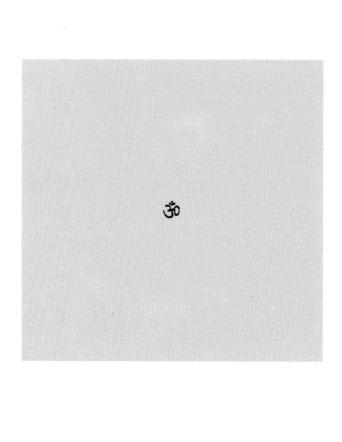

I

DAWN AND BIRTH

The first part of the anthology deals with the invisible foundations of reality. It speaks neither of that which "is" nor of that which "shall be". It uses a past tense, but it does not refer properly to a temporal "was". The origin of time cannot be temporal.

The primordial Word is not yet spoken, nor is the Lord manifested as sovereign; he is not yet the Lord. Our attention is directed toward discovering the role of nothingness, or becoming aware of the place of a void which cannot be said to exist but which makes it possible that things can exist by the very act of filling up the void.

It is an attempt to give expression to God-above-God, the Beginning-before-Life. The prelude is really before the whole play, before all *līlā*, human and divine. It is actually not played: the whole thrust is on what is being unfolded before our eyes. Liberation lies ahead; there is a long way to go. The dawn is not the day, nor is birth really human life, but without them there would be neither day nor our life. The true "be-coming" is an authentic *coming to be*; but do not ask where it comes from lest you stop the very becoming. Without faith nothing takes shape or comes into being. Faith is the

beginning of salvation, because it is the very dawn of
our true being, the essential openness of our human
existence - the very condition of any real, that is, sacred
act, the *Veda* will say.

HYMN TO PRELUDE

ādi

In the beginning, to be sure, nothing existed,
neither the heaven nor the earth nor space in between.
So Nonbeing, having decided to be, became spirit and
said: "Let me be!" He warmed himself further and
from this heating was born fire. He warmed himself
still further and from this heating was born light!
TB II, 2, 9, 1-2

Numerous texts are to be found in the vedic scriptures,
of extraordinary diversity and incomparable richness,
which seek unweariedly to penetrate the mystery of
the beginning and to explain the immensity and the
amazing harmony of the universe. These tests seem to
burst forth impetuously like streams issuing from the
glaciers of Himālayas.

What is fascinating about the experience of the vedic
seers is that not only they have dared to explore the
outer space of being and existence, exploring the
boundaries of the universe, but that they have also
undertaken the risky and intriguing adventure of going
beyond and piercing the being barrier so as to float in

utter nothingness, so to speak, and discover that Nonbeing is only the outer atmosphere of Being, its protective veil. They plunge thus into a darkness enwrapped by darkness, into the Beyond from which there is no return, into that prelude of existence in which there is neither Being nor Nonbeing, neither God nor Gods, nor creature of any type; only Void, the absolute One from which life emerges.

Life emerges in and around us, on the cosmic plane and on the human level. The passage from the darkness of night to the light of life is long and painful, passes through solitude, sacrifice and integration, as the myth of Prajāpati tells us.

Prajāpati having created the world out of the self-sacrifice, is exausted, feeble, on the point of death. He is no longer powerful and mighty; the universe has the possibility of escaping the power of God; it stands on its own. "Once engendered, the creatures turned their backs upon him and went away." They try to free themselves from the creator, but fall into chaos and disorder. If the universe has to subsist, God has to come again and penetrate the creatures afresh, entering into them for a second time. This second redeeming act, however, needs the collaboration of the creature. Here is the locus for Man's collaboration with the unique act of Prajāpati, which gives consistency and existence to the world. This is Man's place and function in the sacrifice.

This sacrifice is not just a kind of offering to God but the action by which we create and procreate along

with God and reconstruct his Body. This action gathers
the first material for the total *yajña* (sacrifice), not from
animals, flowers, or whatever, but from the inmost depth
of Man himself. It is the outcome of Man's urge to be
in tune with that cosmic dynamism which enables
constantly to win over the power of Nonbeing. "That I
may become everything!" says Prajāpati, but it is the
cry that every Man will feel in face of the limitation of
his own person and the small field of action in which
he can operate. When beginning to enter into the poised
state of contemplation, when at peace with himself and
at the threshold of realization, Man has this tremendous
desire to become this and that, to be involved in every
process and to be present everywhere. It is not so much
the hankering for power which drives Man, but, on the
contrary, the existential desire to be active at the very
core of reality, in the divine centre itself whence all
emerges and is directed. "Let me have a self" is another
refrain. The wise Man, described time and again in the
śruti, is not the escapist and unfriendly solitary, but the
full Man who, having realized his own limitations,
knows how to enter into the infinite ocean of *sat, cit*,
and *ānanda*: of being, consciousness, and joy.

The fascination with light bursting forth from the
cosmos is heightened in the speculation of the
Upaniṣad, where the Spirit is named Light. A vision
of the dawn is not an experience of the sun. At dawn
you cannot say where the earth begins and where the
sky ends, where the light dispels darkness or where

the darkness has still the upper hand: all remains a message, an expectation, a promise.

Dawn, Uṣas, is the Goddess of hope and of faith, *bhakti*.

HYMN TO DAWN

Uṣas

Dawn is "beloved" of Heaven:
Just as a young man follows his beloved,
so does the Sun, the Dawn, that shining Goddess
RV I, 115, 2

Resplendent with light, she drives away darkness:

Fresh from her toilet, conscious of her beauty,
she emerges visible for all to see.
Dawn, daughter of Heaven, lends us her lustre,
dispersing all shadows of malignity
RV V, 80, 5

Arousing from deep slumber all that lives,
stirring to motion Man and beast and bird.
RV, IV, 51, 5

5. She wakes to action all who repose in slumber.
Some rise to labor for wealth, others to worship.
Those who saw little before now see more clearly.
Dawn raises to consciousness all living creatures.

7. The daughter of Heaven now appears before us,
a fair young woman clothed in shining garments.
Auspicious Dawn, mistress of earthly treasure,
shine upon us today in queenly splendor.

16. Arise! The breath of life again has reached us.
Darkness has fled and light is fast approaching.
She leaves a pathway for the Sun to travel.
We have arrived where life will again continue.
Mother of Gods and brightness of the Godhead
token of sacrifice, shine forth on high.
Rise up and look upon our prayers with favor.
Bless us among people, Dawn ever desired!
RV I, 113

HYMN TO BIRTH

prathamaṃ janma

As the earth bears fire in her womb
and the heaven is pregnant with lightning
and the quarters have wind as their seed,
so I place in you, my wife, this child.
BU VI, 4, 22

In a Man this [ātman] first becomes a germ,
and this semen is his essence taken from all his limbs;
in himself, indeed, he carries the Self.

When he fecundates a woman, then he causes [a child]
to be born.
This is his first birth.
AU II, 1

II

GERMINATION AND GROWTH

The first part of this anthology describes the appearance of Life on earth and in heaven.

In the second part we shall watch the growth of Consciousness in Man into self-consciousness. Consciousness is not necessarily self-conscious. In the whole of the first part Man's consciousness was alert and very much alive, but Man had not fully realized that it was he who was conscious.

Now Man becomes conscious that he is that pole of universe which recognizes itself to be something other than the centre. But even if God is the centre of the universe and bigger than Man, nevertheless He is God for Man and turns around him like the great and powerful sun that seems to rotate around the tiny earth. Henceforward the dialogue between these two poles will not cease: only the polarity that does not destroy unity will allow for growth and for the unhampered manifestation of reality. This intuition would seem to point out to the work of the Spirit.

Man becomes conscious of the existence of the universe as a hierarchical whole consisting of all sorts of gifts: Gods, men, animals, other beings, spirits, souls, the temporal and the timeless. A very special place is occupied by food, that life stuff that is material and spiritual at the same time, human, divine, and even cosmic, for everything in the universe "eats". Furthermore, the law of eating is so central that not only does everything eat, but all things eat one another, eating being the symbol of the solidarity of the whole universe. We all grow together, we all eat one another. A famous stanza says:

I am food, I am food, I am food!
I, who am food, eat the eater of food.
TU III, 10, 6

This part deals with human consciousness in its most immediate form: the discovery of love and of the human person, which implies initiation and marriage. There is no human growth without this coming of age. These acts are simultaneously both cosmic and human, but the human aspect patently becomes more and more important; the centre of gravity is being shifted from the cosmic to the human. The world of Man does not consist only simply in what he does, but in what he enjoys, that is, in everything that contributes toward a harmonious, civilized, and happy life. Though work is not considered unworthy of Man, yet it is not the highest of human activities.

A striking feature of the vedic revelation is the way in which its secular character in no way undermines the sacredness of life. Divine Providence is more than just a benign surveillance; it is fundamentally a directing of the growth of all creatures, each according to its nature. Let us quote some passages:

O God, you are our providence, our Father.
We are your brothers, you our Source of life.
You are called Father, caring for the humble;
supremely wise, you teach the simple wisdom.
RV I, 31, 10. 14

The One who is the life spark of the waters
of wood, of things both moving and inert,
who has his dwelling even within the stone,
immortal God, he cares for all mankind.
RV I, 70, 2

He who sees all beings at a glance,
both separate and united,
may be our protector!
RV III, 62, 9

The vedic concept of providence seems to emphasize the aspects of protection and nurture. The function of God is not primarly to judge, but to protect, to help us to thrive and flourish.

O God, grant us of boons the best,
a mind to think and a smiling love,
increase of wealth, a healthy body,

speech that is winsome and days that are fair.
RV II, 21, 6

The main thrust of this type of mantra is to awaken the
consciousness that life itself is a gift, and that all that comes
with it or that makes it really alive, and thus worth living is
a gift.

This type of hymn stresses cosmic solidarity in a
markedly anthropological way. Men fight one another,
but then they discover that both sides are invoking the
same God; they tend to think of themselves as the centre
of the universe, and then they realize that the breath of
life, *prāṇa,* is common to all living beings; they are
really united when they look in the same direction,
contemplating the marvels of the divine.

The discovery of time brings with it a realization
that it is like a net that not only draws together the
different moments of a Man's life but also ties him up
with all other temporal creatures. Man may, furthermore,
experience a depth in his own being which does not
belong to the sphere of temporal reality: all are blessings
of the Lord. The fundamental meaning of a blessing is,
perhaps, that it comunicates life by means of an action,
generally embodied in word or gesture. Recognition
and acceptance of the fact there is a blessing at the
source of all that we are and have and do are both signs
of an already mature spirituality.

THE BREATH OF LIFE.

prāṇa

Wind, Breath and Life form a triad which some millenia ago Man experienced as a whole, as deeply related and belonging together. Movement is a common feature of all three. Movement is the soul, that is, the life-principle of every phenomenon in the three worlds. Wind is not just air, but air in movement. Breath is this same movement of the air within living beings. Life is intrinsically movement; it is something that somehow moves without being moved. The experience takes place at a deeper level of reality, a level where that fatal dichotomy between matter and spirit has not yet occured.

Life is an all-pervasive vector in the structure of reality. Something without life is dead, that is, is nonbeing. The wind reveals to us how alive the earth is. Breath discloses to us the intimate connection between life and matter. Life itself is a mere abstraction if there is no living being. But being too is nothing if it is not be-ing, that is, alive.

The hymn given here, dedicated to *prana,* combines in a masterly way all the different aspects of this worldview. This breath of life is the symbol of life itself, that is, life as it manifests itself in living beings. For this very reason it is also death and fever, the rain, the

sun and the moon, and is not separated from the Father
of all beings. Does not life require death in order to
assert itself? Would there be Being if there were no
Source witnessing its very be-ing, its flow?

A difficult line in the last stanza seems to suggest
that the mystery of personal consciousness is bound
up with the identification of the person with this same
Breath of Life: "I am that very Life. I pray that I may
clasp to myself this very Breath of Life, so that I may
live: You are indeed I." The conquest of immortality is
the realization both that life is Life, thus that it does not
die, and also that I *am* insofar as I realize my own
identity with Life.

1. Praise to the Breath of Life!
He rules this world,
master of all things,
on which all things are based.

5. When Breath of Life the broad earth
with rain bedews,
the cattle exult:
"We shall have plenty", they say.

7. Praise to you, Breath, when you come
and praise when you go!
When you stand up
and when you sit still, to you praise!

10. Breath of Life clothes all beings with care
as a father his son;
master of all things,
whether they breathe or breathe not.

14. A Man breathes in, he breahtes out,
within the womb.
Quickened by you,
to birth he comes once more.

15. The mighty Wind they call him, or Breeze.
The future and the past
exist in him.
On Breath of Life all things are based.

24. Of all that is born is he Lord,
of all that moves.
Untiring he, steadfast;
may my prayer bring Breath to my aid!

25. Erect he keeps watch among the sleeping.
He falls not prone.
None ever heard
that he among the sleepers should slumber.

26. Breath of Life, do not forsake me.
You are, indeed, I.
Like the Embryo of the Waters
I bind you to me that I may live!
AV XI, 4

PRAYER FOR HAPPINESS

svastyayana

*We invoke him, the Lord of what moves and what
moves not,
the inspirer of our thoughts. May he come to our aid!
May this our divine protector and guard,
the unfailing one, cause our wealth to increase,
that we may long fluorish!*
RV I, 89, 5

*Blessing and joy to our mother and father!
Joy to cattle, to beasts, and to men!
May all well-being and graces be ours!
Long may we see the sun!*
AV I, 31, 4

Man may possess everything: health, wealth, wife
and children, knowledge and skill, power and glory, but
his happiness, his fullness is incomplete without the
greatest gift: *śānti*. The *śānti* mantra or invocation of
peace is an essential utterance at any beginning, and
especially at the end of a sacred action or of the recitation
of a sacred text. Man and earth affects each other and, at
the same, they both interact with the world of the Gods.
Man is the powerful mediator, because he alone is
capable of uttering the prayer for peace. Peace in heaven,
on earth and in human heart is the meaning of the
threefold wish: *śāntiḥ, śāntiḥ, śāntiḥ!*

III

BLOSSOMING AND FULLNESS

The third part illustrates a basic insight of the whole vedic revelation: reality is lightsome; light pervades everything and makes everything light and joyful. One has only to see. Light is the very structure of reality. This light is, first of all and above all, an aspect of the celestial world but the same cosmic splendor can be found in Man. Man discovers thus his own nature which is both divine and human.

The awakening of human consciousness is not only the chief marvel of creation; it is also the most formidable adventure of Man who discovers to be partner of God himself, a pole of an unbreakable relation, and the burden of this consciousness leads him to discover not only the laws of sacrifice but also its nature. Man may enter into the mystery of reality only by an existential and total involvement of his being which will consume him in the very fire of the sacrifice: the one who emerges will be a risen person, a new being. God is Light, the *ātman* is Light, and so the Man who has realized the *ātman* is self-luminous and radiant.

THE INNER LIGHT

ātmajyotis

Glory to God the shining.
Protect me from death.
Glory to God the resplendent,
the first cause of all.

May the Sun in the East, may the Sun in the West,
may the Sun in the North, may the Sun in the South,
may the Sun give perfect life,
with long life endow us.
SuryU 71

6. The Sun, when rising, enters the eastern regions and
gathers in his beams all the breath of life that is in the
east. When he illumines the other regions, the south, the
west, and the north, below, above, and in between, then
he gathers in his beams the whole of breath of life.

7. Thus arises the Sun as Fire, the universal Life-Breath
which assumes every form.
PrasnU I, 6-7

The early morning light we see
emerging from the primordial seed
and gleaming higher than the heaven.
And from the darkness that surrounds us,
gazing upon the highest heaven,

we attain to the Sun, the God of Gods,
the highest Light, the highest Light.
CU III, 17, 7

There is a Light that shines above this heaven, above
all worlds, above everything that exists in the highest
worlds beyond which there are no higher- this is the
Light that shines within Man.
CU III, 13, 7

Even as the radiance of the Sun
enlightens all regions, above, below,
and slantwise, so that only God,
glorious and worthy of worship, rules
over all his creation.
SU V, 4

THE FIRE SACRIFICE

agnihotra

Without light there is no life; light is sun and fire.
Agnihotra, the offer of fire, is the quintessence of
sacrifice. This simple, essential rite is performed in the
morning and in the evening: Man is the sacrificer and
the sacrifice, the cosmic priest as well as the cosmic
victim.

Light is Agni, Agni is light. The one who is light, he
calls light...

*Agni offers itself in sacrifice to the rising Sun
and the setting Sun offers itself in sacrifice to Agni in
the evening.*

*Night sacrifices itself to the Day and Day sacrifices
itself to the Night.*
KausB II, 8

SACRIFICE IS MAN
puruṣayajña

*The sacrifice is Man. It is Man [who offers it] because
it is Man who spreads it out and because, in being
spread out, it assumes exactly the same stature as Man.
For this reason, the sacrifice is Man.*
SB I, 3, 2, 1

THE SACRIFICE OF THE MIND
mānasayajña

*Where there is duality, there one sees another, one
smells another, one tastes another, one speaks to
another, one hears another, one knows another; but
where everything has become one's own Self, with what
should one see whom, with what should one smell
whom, with what should one test whom, with what
should one speak to whom, with what should one hear
whom, with what should one think of whom, with what*

should one touch whom, with what should one know whom? How can He be known by whom all this is made known? He, the Self, is not this, not this. He is ungraspable for He is not grasped. He is indestructible for he cannot be destroyed, He is unattached for He does not cling [to anything]. He is unbound, He does not suffer nor is he injured. Indeed, by whom should the Knower be known? By these words, Maitreyī, you have been instructed. Such, in truth, is immortality.
BU IV, 5, 15

1. Just as fire without fuel is extinguished in its own source, so is the mind estinguished in its own source, when thoughts have ceased.

3. The mind indeed is this fleeting world; therefore it should be purified with great effort. One becomes like that which is in one's mind - this is the everlasting secret.

6. The mind has been declared to be of two kinds: pure and impure. It becomes impure when it is touched by desire, and pure when freed from desire.

7. When a man, having made his mind perfectly stable, free from attachment and confusion, enters upon the mindless state, then he attains the supreme abode.

9. The bliss that arises in the state of highest absorption, when the pure mind has come to rest in the Self, can

*never be expressed by words! One must experience it
directly, one's own self, in one's inner being.*

*10. If a man's mind is merged in the Self, then he is
completely released, just as water is not distinguishable
in Water, or fire in Fire, or air in Air.*
MaitU VI, 34

THE INTEGRAL ACTION

karmayoga

*Action is pure when it is performed with renunciation
of its fruits.*
*Brahman is all: the act of offering,
the offerer and the fire!*
*He who concentrates on Brahman in all his actions
shall surely reach Brahman.*
BG IV, 24

*Therefore, always perform with detachment
the work you must do;
only by work performed with detachment
does Man reach the highest.*
BG III, 19

IV

FALL AND DECAY

In the fourth stage Man begins to discover that also within himself there is a lack of harmony or, in in the words of the *Gītā*, that there is something obstructing his own will and compelling him to sin. He experiences failure not only because he suffers from his own limitations, but also because he is often ill-treated by God, attacked by his fellow beings, who exploit, betray and even kill him. No wonder that he will start searching for the Self. Man fails to do what he wants and even feels that he cannot really want what he would like to want. Moreover, he senses the contingency of his own existence, he discovers that there are things and states that are irreparable. There are dreams that cannot be fulfilled and desires that have to be abandoned. There is nothing abnormal in this situation. To grow to maturity means to learn to accept the real human predicament.

In other words, the ecstatic attitude described in the previous parts is here diminished. No one escapes the experience of pain and suffering or the temptation to frustation and even despair. Man looks inward not, first of all, to discover a new and untarnished world, but to solve the riddle of his own self; he is a suffering being, trying to understand what has gone wrong with him, for the results are not what he expected or desired.

Man faces fall and decay. The vedic Man makes a clear distinction between long life and old age. The former is a blessing, the latter a curse; the former is a sign of growth and maturity, the latter the unmistakable sign of fall and decay.

We are touching here one of the central problems of Man's experience, the mystery of human sorrow. Man experiences the decay of his body and his own suffering as something foreign to him, something outside himself, as if it came from the unknown, from another world, so to speak. This suffering is either the scorpion sting of some evil power or the very means through which he discovers his true nature beyond all the entanglements of the human condition. The first myth is represented by the vedic period, and the second is typically upaniṣadic and vedantic, though in fact a too clear-cut distinction would be wrong. In the one case sorrow is that which disturbs the physical as well as the psychic harmony; it is abnormal and external and thus can be overcome only if the causes are properly known and the appropriate remedies applied. In the second case sorrow is the very factor that enables Man to rupture the bonds of his human predicament; the body is not the *ātman*, because the body is mortal whereas the *ātman* is immortal. The desire for the ageless state, free from decay, is nothing other than the search for the immortal *ātman* in Man.

BEYOND SORROW AND SUFFERING
vītaśoka

"Sir, how is it possible to enjoy one's desires in this body [of ours] which is ill-smelling, unsubstantial, a heap of bone, skin, muscle, marrow, flesh, semen, blood, mucus, tears, rheum, feces, urine, wind, bile, and phlegm? How is it possible to enjoy one's desires in this body, afflicted as it is with desire, anger, greed, delusion, fear, frustration, envy, separation from what one longs for and association with what one abhors, hunger, thirst, old age, death, disease, sorrow, and similar things?"
MaitU I, 3

13. He who has found and awakened to the ātman which has entered the otherwise impenetrable body, he is the maker of the universe, of all things. The world is his! The world itself is he!

14. This we may know, indeed, while here on earth. If we do not know it, great is the destruction. But those who know it become immortal. The others attain only distress.
BU IV, 13-14

PURIFYING KNOWLEDGE

jñānaśuddhi

May the word, the mind, the eye, the ear,
the tongue, the nose, the semen, the intelligence,
the intention, and the will be purified in me!
I am light! May I be purified from all stain and sin!
MahanarU 441

From the dark I go to the colored, from the colored to
the dark. Shaking off sin as a horse shakes off dust
from its hair, freeing myself from the body as the moon
frees itself from the mouth of Rāhu, I enter into the
unmade world of Brahman with a fulfilled ātman. I
enter into the world of Brahman.
CU VIII, 13, 1

When a Man knows God all fetters are loosened.
Sorrows are no more; birth and death cease.
By meditation on him, at the bodyís dissolution,
there comes the third state, that of supreme mastery.
His desires are fullified; he is absolutely free.
SU 1, 11

The Fire of Wisdom

jñānāgni

*As a blazing fire reduces the wood
to ashes, O Arjuna,
so does the fire of knowledge reduce
all activity to ashes
BG IV, 37*

*To you who have faith I will tell a deep mystery
that holds within itself
both vision and knowledge. By knowing this mystery
you will be freed from all evil.
BG IX, 1*

*Concentrating on Me, you shall overcome
by my grace all dangers;
but if from self-conceit you will not listen,
you will surely perish.
BG XVIII, 58*

V

DEATH AND DISSOLUTION

To desire to live and not to desire at the same degree death that life may contain is not a realistic desire to live but a mere product of our imagination, which seeks to grasp at an illusory" life". The vedic attitude, which is strongly life-affirming, has as its corollary the acceptance of death.

Modern Man wonders about death and weaves innumerable theories about it; he seems to be sure about only one thing: its factual reality and thus its inevitability. Modern society tends to wipe out from the memory of the living all dealings with the dying and the dead. The fundamental vedic attitude is almost the opposite: it does not try to smuggle death away from everyday life.

According to this vision, which is common to other cultures as well, death is not inevitable; it is only accidental. You die if your life is snatched away before you reach maturity, preventing you from achieving what you, yourself or society was expecting of your life.

On the other hand the old Man, "the Man of long life", as the *Veda* call him, the one who has lived his life, who has fulfilled his life span, his *āyus,* does not die; he has simply consumed the torch and exhausted the fuel. The flame of his life goes on and it burns in his sons, his daughters, his children's children, his friends, his work, and his ideas which are scattered to the four winds. Only the last gifts of his body and breath still remain to be given away. The old Man does not die; he simply finishes his commerce with life and achieves the trasmission of all that he himself has received, as the *Upaniṣads* describe. That is more convincing for the vedic Man than for the modern Man because of the deeper sense of collective consciousness, which the former enjoys in comparison with contemporary Man.

THE GREAT DEPARTURE
mahāprasthāna

O Indra, prolong our life once more!
RV I, 10, 11

The "afterlife" and the "otherworld" may be very attractive prospects, but nothing is so dear and desiderable as our human, concrete, bodily life here on earth and under the sun, with fellow human beings, animals, and objects surrounding us. If later certain upaniṣadic sages and, more so, some of their followers despise life here below and all human values, the vedic *ṛṣis* are still in love with this world.

Just a cucumber is removed from its stalk,
so from Death's bonds may I be removed
but not from immortality!
RV VII, 59, 12

The poet of this stanza knows only too well that death
does not wait for the fruit to fall from the tree by itself
through its own impulse. He uses the metaphor of the
plucked fruit and asks to be saved from the embrace of
death and handed over to immortality. The cucumber
dies when plucked; Man enters immortality.
Desireless, wise, immortal, self-existent,
full of bliss, lacking in nothing,
is the one who knows the wise, unaging,
youthful ātman: he fears not death!
AV X, 8, 44

The stanza comes from the always astonishing
Atharva-veda. Composed long before the *Upaniṣads,*
it introduces us to the concept of *ātman,* the discovery
of which is the one means of overcoming both death
and the fear of death. The three verses chosen as
antiphons for this section express the gist of the many
texts concerning what the *Kaṭha-upaniṣad* calls the
"Great departure".

Within Death there is Immortality

Antaraṃ mṛtyor amṛtam

Death does not die and thus within death itself there is immortality. Here is something more than what we learn from the *Upaniṣads,* that "life does not die".

We are not satisfied with discovering a *jīva,* a soul resistant to the bite of death; we hear that death itself belongs to immortality, that death is not the "end" of life, not something frightening on the frontier, but a constitutive element of life itself.

Death is not at the limit of life, but in the middle of it. The very universality of death makes Man give it a superhuman character, and thus it acquires a quasi-divine status.

On this point there is a verse:

"Within Death there is immortalilty", for after Death comes immortality. "On Death is based immortality", for it is within immortality that the person established in yonder orb shines. "Death clothes itself in Light", for Light, to be sure, is yonder Sun, because this light changes day and night, and so Death clothes itself in Light and is surrounded on all sides by Light, "The Self of Death is in the Light", for the Self of that person is assuredly in that orb.
SB X, 5, 2,4

Man, at the hour of his death, certainly becomes one; that is, he simplifies his life, he discards what is merely accidental and, in particular, he concentrates and condenses his whole being so that what he leaves behind or passes on to others is the very core of his being, the kernel of his person, the *ātman,* which will not fade away. Thus death is the supreme act.

Liturgy of the Rite of Purification.

The priest chants:

From unreality lead me to reality;
from darkness lead me to light
from death lead me to immortality.
BU I, 3, 28

VI

NEW LIFE AND FREEDOM

What is real immortal life? Certainly not the clinging to a continuation of mortal life. True life cannot die, but it implies not only the transformation of the object "life" but also the transformation of the "living" subject. This radical metamorphosis is liberation (*mokṣa*).

What is a full and authentic life and how may we reach it?

The vedic experience is one of liberation, of freedom from everything. It thus includes freedom or liberation from time. What both fascinates and haunts upaniṣadic Man is not anything that comes after, but that which has no after.

Man has to break the circularity of time in order to reach the ontological fullness of his being. To enter into this other atemporal, but no less real, sphere is to attain realization, to reach liberation, from the encirclement of time and freedom from temporal chains. It is a truly new life, not in the sense of a "recycled" life but in the sense of a new type, a new kind of life, indeed, the only real and authentic life.

The way to the "new life" is a long and a complex one.

The *Upaniṣads* are about the disclosure of this experience, which leads to the freedom, to the fullness.

The Ascending Way

brahmajñāna

That is Fullness, this is Fullness,
from Fullness comes Fullness.
When Fullness is taken from Fullness,
Fullness remains.
BU V,1

"Man is on pilgrimage to his *ātman*". In this pilgrimage Man sets out to find the oneness of all things and discovers, as he proceeds, the tool by which such a search is undertaken: consciousness. Oneness and consciousness are the two landmarks on the ascending way.

The goal of the pilgrimage is the knowledge of Brahman, the total *jñāna*, the perfect and conscious realization of what Brahman is: the real, the truth, the One.

What is the nature of reality ? How is the One itself constituited so that there is place for plurality without destroying the unity? Is there anything that allows for movement, distinctions, life, without endangering the One? What kind of plurality can coexist with oneness?

Consciousness and consciousness alone is able to assume multiplicity without endangering oneness. In the world of human experience, consciousness is the only power that embraces the manifold without losing its identity and unity. Consciousness can be aware of the many without being split into multiplicity.

The discovery of pure conscious represents a radical departure from the first natural movement of our being. It implies the reversion of the natural movement towards the object, towards the other, and it entails a direction towards the subject, towards the knower.

The discourse on Brahman starts from the discovery that pure consciousness is not self-consciousness. Brahman is not the object of consciousness, or even the subject. Brahman is pure consciousness: pure consciousness has no support. Brahman is not a substance. Brahman *has* no consciousness, and thus no self-consciousness. Brahman *is* consciousness.

Men *have* consciousness, they are conscious beings, but they are not (yet?) consciousness and much less pure consciousness. The sole consciousness that exists is an all-encompassing consciousness; it is Brahman.

One *Upaniṣad* says:
That from which beings are born,
that by which, when born, they live,
that into which, when dying, they enter,
that you should desire to know:
that is Brahman.
TU III, 1

This Brahman, source and end of everything, is not a separated "being", is not merely at the beginning and

end of the ontic pilgrimage: Brahman is consciousness.
We are insofar as we are in and from Brahman. He is
the ultimate Oneness of reality. He is the subtle center
of our existence, that is, consciousness (*cit*), and also
the ultimate joy and bliss (*ānanda*). The later vedantic
definition of Brahman as *sat* (being), *cit* (consciousness),
and *ānanda* (bliss) is foreshadowed in the *Upaniṣads*
in various ways, but the stress is always on "knowing",
on realizing the unknowable as it is hidden in one's
heart, for to know it is to become it. And the goal of
upaniṣadic knowledge is nothing less than the
attainment of this state of being which is the being of
Brahman itself.

As another *Upaniṣad* says:

"*It is in truth that Imperishable, who is not seen but
is the seer, who is not heard but is the hearer, who is
not thought but is the thinker, who is not known, but
is the knower. There is no other seer but him, no
other hearer but him, no other thinker but him, no
other knower but him. And it is that Imperishable
which is the warp and the woof of space.*"
BU III, 8, 11

*Brahman is consciousness and joy,
the highest reward of the offerer of gifts
and of the one who stands still and knows.*
BU III, 9, 28

1. Revealed and yet dwelling hidden in the cave
is that which is called the great Abode.
Whatever moves and breathes and blinks
is fixed therein. Know this as being
and also nonbeing, the desire of all hearts,
transcending knowledge, best beloved of every creature.
2. Burning as a flame and subtlest of the subtle,
in which are firmly fixed the worlds and all their
peoples-
that is the imperishable Brahman. That is life
and word and spirit, the true, the immortal!
That, my friend, is to be known – know that!
MundU II, 2, 1-2

THE INTERNAL WAY

puruṣo 'ntarātmā

The *ātman* must be realized and its identity with
Brahman discovered: an injunction that is repeated
again and again. It is not a question of finding an
objectified *ātman* but of realizing it. To recognize the
equation amounts to discover that trascendence has no
real meaning except in relation to immanence. The
water of the drop becomes the water of the ocean when
merges into it, but the ocean is not the drop.

The equation *ātman-brahman* cannot be grasped by
an intellectual approach, but only by an act of grace,
by a "choice" on the part of the *ātman*. But to receive

this grace requires purity of life and mind, concentration and interior peace.

One should meditate on the ātman which consists of spirit, whose embodiment is life, whose form is light, whose essence is space, which changes its form at will, swift as thought, of true resolve and true stability; which contains all odors, all tastes, pervades all regions and encompasses the whole world, speechless and indifferent.
Like a grain of rice or barley or millet, like a tiny grain of millet, so is the golden Person within the ātman. Like smokeless flame, greater than heaven, greater than the atmosphere, greater than the earth, greater than all beings, he is the ātman of life, my own ātman. On departing [from this world] I shall become that ātman. He who has this confidence, he shall not waver. This was spoken, and it is truly so.
SB X, 6, 3, 2

That which breathes with your breath, that is your ātman which is within everything. That which exhales with your exhalation, that is your ātman which is within everything. That which breathes diffusedly with your diffused breath, that is your ātman which is within everything. That which breathes up with your up-breath, that is your ātman which is within everything. This, in truth, is your aṃtman which is within everything.
BU III, 4, 1

THE DISCLOSURE OF THE SUBJECT
aham-brahman

The passage from *brahman-ātman* to *aham-brahman*
[I (am) *brahman*] is a capital one.

The question "what or who is the *ātman*?" must turn
into "who am I?" It is here that *neti, neti* enters upon the
scene: not this, not that. Nothing answers the question
adequately. I am not my body (only), I am not my mind
(alone), I am not (exclusively) what I am today or was
yesterday or shall be tomorrow. We are not asking what
the I *is*, but searching out who I *am,* who I am in the
deepest recesses of my being, who I ultimately am as
mover and knower and being or whatever. It is obvious
that this ultimate I can in no way be identified with a
psychological ego.

The I that can say "I am" is the only real and true I.
Only the realized Man can say in truth *aham-brahman.*

I

aham

The first awakening of consciousness finds its
spontaneous expression in the words "I am", *aham
asmi. Aham*, I, is thus the first word, the first name, as
the same *Upaniṣad* says, not only of the primordial
ātman, but of every Man. But it is also Man's last word.

Only then, having reached the I, does Man attain immortality and thus depart from this earth. It is the full consciousness of the "I" (which is the opposite of egoistic self-centeredness) which frees Man from all fears. Only the consciousness of the "I" is real freedom.

If in the beginning there was the "I am", the pure awareness of the "I" will also be at the end of the human pilgrimage. There is but one basic difference. It is the realized Man who discovers his ultimate identity with the *puruṣa,* with the *aham.* Making this discovery is what constitutes human life on earth, the real process of human growth. The *Maitrī- Upaniṣad* expands the thought that this oneness with and of the One, Brahman, is realized only by the realization of the "I". The *aham* is the principle of unity even in the Absolute.

In the beginning Brahman was alone, but the moment He realized his aloneness He opened up his own existence, as it were. He cried as in wonder, *"I am brahman!"* and in this consciousness he opened up the possibility of existence for the entire universe. Communication was made possible; communion appeared; the relation was installed and with it the existence of reality. Between *Brahman* and *aham-Brahman* lies the entire temporal universe.

The only possible utterance of the *aham* is *Brahman.* I *am* neither body (alone) nor mind (only) nor creature (exclusively) nor God (uniquely) - *I am* certainly all this as well as much more: *aham Brahman.* For this reason the only spontaneous attitude of the Man to whom this revelation dawns is to cry *I offer myself in oblation.*

12. Neither by the word nor by the mind
nor by sight can ever be reached.
How, then, can He be realised
except by exclaiming, "He is"?

13. One must realize him first as "He is"
and then also his existential nature.
When realized as the "He is",
then he shows his existential nature.
KathU VI, 12-13

What am I? I am Brahman!
Yes, I am Brahman, I am!
I verily offer myself in oblation!
MahanarU 157-158

In me alone originates the All,
in me the All is established,
in me all things come to rest.
I am that Brahman without a second!
KaivU 19

THE ENCOUNTER

Yoga

Having realized "I am Brahman",
one is released from all bondage.
KaivU 17

Because Brahman is the I, there is place for the you: "that are you", the you of the I, the you of Brahman. This is what we are, a you, nothing more and nothing less; nothing more as without the I we have no consistency or existence; but also nothing less, as we are Brahman, of Brahman, equal to Brahman and have infinite value: *sat, cit, ānanda,* being, spirit, and glory. That is what the great vedic utterance (teaching) affirms.

This intuition entails the great conversion, that is, the reverse of the apparent order of things in order to acquire the true vision of reality. It requires from us a change of the heart, just as it also demands the change of object into subject and vice versa, the overcoming of egocentrism, and the recovery of the true you-character of the creature. It represents a radical change of perspective: we are a *you* and the you has meaning only for the I and existence only from the I. The you is only "be-ing", that is, a response, thanksgiving, and love. According to this intuition, our proper relationship with the Supreme is not one of *I-you*, but just the opposite, one of *you-I*. The Absolute or Brahman or God (or any other word we may prefer) is not the you

(whom we may pray or think of) but the I, and we are
his you. This personal aspect makes room for the total
development of my being and my person.

Now Śvetaketu is receiving the culmination of the
teaching from his father who says to him: "that are you",
tat tvam asi.

"That is *ātman,* that is Brahman, that is reality."
Now, that which you are, which is in you, resides in
you, that is *tvam,* a you, the you. It is not a different
thing, it is not another "that", it is your you. You are,
Śvetaketu, not an undiscriminated part of the universe.
You are the *you* of Brahman, the partner of Brahman,
not different from him and much less separated, you
are his other pole, his tension, his "person", as we might
cautiously add.

The human being is a person because he is a you
and he emerges as a person, not when he begins to feel
or to know objects but when he realizes that he is being
loved, known, watched, sought, and cared for.
Personhood arises with you-awareness.

Śvetaketu, you are a person, a human person, a you;
you are inasmuch as you are loved, known, produced,
by the I, inasmuch as you respond to this call, to this
act of the I. You are not the I, Śvetaketu, there is only
one I capable of saying in truth "I am", *aham-asmi,* I
am *brahman, aham brahman.* This is the supreme
ātman . It resides in you, is you, and is you in such a
way that only by realizing it you can become you,
your-self.

Tat tvam asi: tat, Brahman, is a *tvam,* a you in you.
You are a you of Brahman. This is possible precisely
because *ātman-brahman,* that is, because the *he,* which
you have discovered as being the I, that *ātman,* which
has been disclosed, revealed to you as Brahman, is,
has a you in you: otherwise you would not be. But you
are, you are a you, the bridge between the *ātman* and
brahman, the link that unites and identifies them. It is
this discovery of pure consciousness which makes this
possible, because neither are you without the I nor is
He without you. And it is this realization of yours which
makes you emerge as a *tvam,* a you which is not duality,
but the very expression of the aduality of the *ekam,* of
the One.

The whole of reality subsists in this relational or
personal structure. Brahman, the nature of which is pure
consciousness is the unique and ultimate *I* which exists
precisely because it has a *you*, which responds to its
own constitutive calling by responding via the *ātman,*
without splitting the pure oneness of all. This stretching
of the aduality, this tension and polarity within the One,
making it really adual but without breaking its oneness,
is precisely the mistery of life disclosed in the
Upaniṣads, whose climax is found in the experience
of *tat tvam asi.*

YOU

Uddālaka Aruṇi spoke to his son Śvetaketu:

"All living beings, my dear, have their root in Being, have their resting place in Being, have their support in Being."

...

"This body dies, when deprived of life, but life does not die. That which is this finest element the whole word has for its self. That is trmuth; that is the ātman; that are you, Śvetaketu!"

"Let me earn even more, sir!"

"Very well, my dear!, he said"

"Bring me a fruit of the fig tree!"

"Here it is, sir."

"Break it open!"

"There it is, sir!"

"What do you see?"

"These fine seeds, like tiny particles."

"Break one open!"

"There it is, sir."

"What do you see?"

"Nothing at all, sir!" said Śvetaketu

The father said to him:

"Believe me, my dear! The finest element, which you cannot perceive out of this finest element, my dear, comes this big fig tree!

"That which is this finest element, the whole world has for its self: That is truth; that is the ātman; that are you, Śvetaketu!"

"Let me learn more, sir!"

"Very well, my dear,"he said.

"Put this salt in the water and come to me again tomorrow morning."

He did so.

Then he said to him:

"Bring the salt that you put in the water last evening."
When he searched for it, he could not find it, for it was all dissolved.

"Taste the water on this side! How does it taste?"
"Salty."

"Taste the water from the middle; How does it taste?"
"Salty."

"Taste from that side! How does it taste?"
"Salty."

"Taste once more and come to me."
He did so, (saying) "it is always the same."

Then his father said to him:

"In the same way you do not perceive Being here, although it is always present."

"That which is the finest element, the whole world has for its self: That is the truth; that is ātman; that are you, Śvetaketu!"

...

Thereupon he realized, yes, he realized.
CU VI, 8-14

You are in truth the visible Brahman.
I will proclaim you as the visible Brahman.
I will speak the right, I will speak the truth.
May this protect me, may it protect my teacher!
May this protect me, may it protect my teacher!
OM peace, peace, peace!
TU I, 1

Now this has been said elsewhere: The body is the bow, the syllabe OM is the arrow, the mind is its tip, darkness is the goal. Piercing darkness one reaches that which is not wrapped in darkness. Piercing that which is wrapped in darkness one beholds Brahman–as it were a sparkling wheel of fire, of the color of the sun, powerful, beyond darkness, the Brahman that shines in yonder sun, in the moon, in fire, and in lightning. Having seen him, one enters upon immortality. Thus it is said:

Inward-directed contemplation on the Highest
is often deflected to outside objects.
Unqualified understanding thus becomes qualified.
But the happiness obtained when the mind is absorbed
has only the ātman as witness.
That is Brahman, the pure, the immortal,
that is the goal, that certainly is the world!
MaitU VI, 24

That which is the supreme Brahman
the ātman of all, the great foundation
of this whole universe, more subtle
than the subltle, eternal ñ that are you!
You are that!
KaivU 16

LIBERATION

Mokṣa

The entire purpose of the *śruti* is liberation or freedom.
Freedom may be interpreted in many ways. It is
Brahman, *ātman, nirvāṇa,* or simply Being, happiness,
release from all bondage. Many are the ways supposed
to lead to it. Right action, true knowledge, and real love
are the classical ways.

The common, fundamental feature of *mokṣa* in the
entire Vedic experience is the simplification, the
elimination, the utter freedom and even unconcern by
which Man can reach his final destination.

I know that Primordial Man, golden as the sun,
beyond darkness. Knowing him a man even now
becomes immortal. This is the way
to attain him; there is no other.
YV XXXI, 18

When he is releazed from all the desires
That bind the heart, then mortal man

Even here becomes immortal and realizes Brahman.
BU IV, 4, 7

His form is not in the field of vision.
No one is able to see him with the eye.
Apprehending him by heart, by thought, and by mind,
Those who know him thus become immortal.

THE SACRED SYLLABLE

Om

This is the syllable of assent, for when one agrees with
something, one says: OM, "yes." That [prayer] to
which assent is made will be fulfilled. He who, knowing
this, meditates upon the Udgītha chant as the syllable
OM will have all his desires fulfilled.
CU I,1,8

A mighty weapon, the Upaniṣad! Take it as a bow.
Affix an arrow, sharpened by devotion.
Bend the bow by a thought concentrated on That.
Hit the target, my dear, the Imperishable!

OM is the bow, the ātman is the arrow;
Brahman, they say, is the target, to be pierced
by concentration; thus one becomes
united with Brahman as an arrow with the target.
MahanarU 540-541

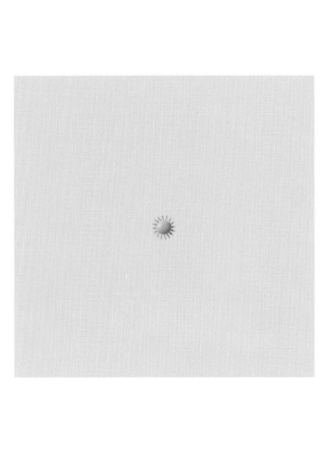

VII

TWILIGHT

Saṁdhyā

The whole universe proceeds on its way. The whole of our personal existence also follows its own path and describes a similar cycle, following and reenacting the divine and the cosmic ones. There is a correspondence between the celestial and terrestrial spheres. Between these two - the sphere of the God or divine reality and the sphere of earthly or cosmic existence - there is yet a third and intermediate sphere: the *antarikṣa*, the region between *dyu* (heaven) and *pṛthivī* (earth). The third sphere is the realm of Man, the mediator between the two. In other words, the *ātman* is the connecting link between this *loka* and the *brahma-loka*.

Within the intermediate sphere there is an "inner shrine; it is this that we should seek" (CU VIII,1,1); it is from here that we contemplate both our own existence and the destiny of the entire reality. It is the sphere of prayer, meditation, contemplation, or simply of personal consciousness.

Consciousness does more than simply reflect that which is. It modifies, to say the least, the thing that it "reflects." Man's conscious existence is not a mere copy or a simple mirroring of that which is, but a

constitutive factor of reality itself. This is the life of the
spirit or the life of prayer. It is not a state of mere
passivity, nor is it a disconnected activity. It is the
marriage, the union, the *maithuna*, between
the two.

Saṁdhyā represents that third sphere which
encompasses our whole life and destiny as well as the
life of the universe; it is the meeting of the lights, of the
morning light with the evening light. It is both the time
of prayer and the prayer of time, for the world could
not subsist if it were only a series of temporal
successions. How would it pass from one instant to the
next if there was no link between the two? This link is
the Spirit, the spirit of prayer that unfolds in the mind
and heart of the enlightened person, of the one who is
rejuvenated by the waters and reborn by the rites of a
second birth.

To be a Man, then, is not only to be a part of the
world but to be the universe itself, as we have already
heard: "the world is his; the world itself is he!" (BU
IV,4,13).

Two practices should be recommended at this point.
The one is utter silence and quiet, emptiness and void,
an active removal of all obstacles in order to let the
Spirit act unhampered; this is the way of absolute
freedom which implies even freedom from being. Here
no word is allowed. It would deform the experience
and, if formulated, would be objectionable. Here "all
words recoil" (TU II,4) or, as another Upaniṣad said,

"*ātman* is silence." The other practice is the traditional prayer of morning and evening, built of praise, human and concrete. It integrates into itself all aspects of human life on earth. God is a partner of Man, not an aloof, mighty power. It is here that the so-called incantations and charms have their place and also efforts at assuring the support of the Gods in battles public or private.

The Godhead has to take some form for me, even if I think of it as a formless "form." It has to have a name, even if it be -nameless. It has to take place somewhere, even if it is in the cave of the heart. It has to take place within a particular time, even if it touches the eternal. The *ista-devatā* concretizes the re-presentation of the Godhead.

The prayers which conclude this anthology were divided in the original book according to the different seasons and the different moments of the day. Here the short selection refers only to prayers to be uttered at sunrise and at sunset.

AT SUNRISE

At dawn Man faces the mistery of the origins: how did men, the cosmos, come to be, come to life? What, who, is behind the scenes? At the rising of the sun a new day starts. The time has come to sacrifice to Agni, pure light, from whom men implore protection from evil and disease.

THE LIGHT OF MAN

Agni

O shining One, cause now the Sun,
that unaging star, to climb the sky,
Imparting light to men.

You, O Lord, are mankind's bright sign,
best, most beloved of the people. Awake!
Give strength to the singer!
RV X, 156, 4-5

THE BURNING LIGHT

Sūrya

Across the expanse of the whole horizon
the seven bay mares draw the Sun on this chariot,
the Lord of each single thing, moving and inert,
to bring us joy.
RV VII, 66, 15

What was the primal matter, what the substance?
How could it be discerned, how was it made?
From which the Designer of all things, beholding all,
fashioned the Earth and shaped the glory of the
Heavens?
RV X, 81, 2

Dawn, Emblem of the Immortal

Uṣas

*O Dawn, whose enterprises never fail
And who understands all things, accept our songs.
O ancient yet ever-youthful Goddess, you proceed
In accordance with Law, endowed with wealth and
fullness.*

*Arising, you turn your face toward all creatures.
You, O Dawn, are the emblem of the Immortal.
You who each day proceed to the same goal,
direct toward us, O Maiden, your chariot.*
RV III, 61, 1-3

Immortality

Amṛta

*To one result leads the impermanent, they say,
to another the permanent. Thus we have heard
from the wise who explained it to us.*

*The Man who understands both the impermanent and
the permanent
holding the two in tension together,
by the impermanent passes over death
and by the permanent attains immortal life.*
IsU 13-14

THE DIVINE FRIEND

Mitra

He who is called Divine Friend brings Men together.
The Divine Friend supports both earth and heaven,
watching over the peoples, never closing an eye.
To the Divine Friend offer an oblation of fatness!
RV III, 59, 1

Unveil Your Face that I May See the Truth!
Satyadharmāya drstaye

The face of Truth is covered over
by a golden vessel. Uncover it, O Lord,
that I who love the truth may see.

O Lord, sole Seer, Controller, Sun,
son of the Father of beings, shine forth.
Concentrate your splendor that I may behold
your most glorious form. He who is yonder-
the Man yonder-I myself am he!

Go, my breath, to the immortal breath.
Then may this body end in ashes!
Remember, O my mind, the deeds of the past,
remember the deeds, remember the deeds!

O Lord, lead us along the right path
to prosperity. O God, you know all our deeds.

Take from us our deceitful sin.
To you, then, we shall offer our prayers.
IsU 15-18

At Sunset

In the evening, when the business of the day has come
to an end, when activities have ceased, men gather
around the light feeling the need for protection, for
security. The flames of Agni enkindles in Man the poetic
inspiration that, going beyond the level of appearances,
penetrates to the very core of reality.

May the Wind Blow Sweetness!

Viśvedevāḥ

May the wind blow sweetness,
the rivers flow sweetness,
the herbs grow sweetness,
for the Man of Truth !

Sweet be the night,
sweet the dawn,
sweet be earthís fragrance,
sweet Father Heaven!

May the tree afford us sweetness,
the sun shine sweetness,
our cows yield sweetness

96   Initiation to the Vedas

milk in plenty!
RV I, 90, 6-8

THE MOON KEEPS WATCH

Varuṇa

The stars fixed on high appear at night.
By day they depart, we know not whither.
Varuṇa's laws are faithful. The moon
sails on at night with a watchful eye.
RV I, 24, 10

THE SELF WITHIN

Antarātman

That by which one perceives form and taste,
perfumes, sounds, and loving caresses,
by that selfsame one knows. What else remains?
This, I now declare, is that!

By knowing as the great all-pervading Self
that by which one is conscious of both
the dream state and also the state of wakefulness,
the wise remain exempt from sorrow!

The one who knows that Self within,
who enjoys like a bee the honey of the spirit,

Lord of what was and what is to be,
will never shrink away from Him.
This, I now declare, is that!

He who was born of old from austerity,
the one who was born of old from the waters,
who enters the cave [of the heart] and dwells there,
This, I now declare, is that!
KathU IV, 3-6

THE GIVER OF GROWTH

Parjanya

May God, the giver of growth to plants,
who holds sways over the waters and all moving
creatures,
grant us threefold protection to guard us
and threefold light to aid and befriend us!.
RV VII, 101, 2

THE CAVE OF THE HEART

Guhā

She who comes into being through the breath of life,
from whom the Gods all took their birth,
the Boundless Goddess of Infinity,
who enters the cave [of the heart] and dwells there
This, I now declare, is that!

Fire the All-Knowing, hidden within the fire sticks
like the seed of life cherished by pregnant women,
worthy of worship daily offered
by reverent men bringing their oblations
This, I now declare, is that!

That from which the sun arises,
into which it sinks to rest,
that in which all the Gods are fixed
and beyond whose reach no one can go
This, I now declare, is that!
KathU IV, 7-9

A LOVING FRIEND

Soma

O God, be happy in our hearts to dwell,
as cows in milk rejoice in grassy meadows,
or as a bridegroom rejoices in his own house!
When in your friendship a mortal finds delight,
then, mighty Sage, you grant him your favor.
Save us, O Lord, from distress and damnation.
Come to us, Lord, as a loving friend!
RV 1, 91,13-15

HE WHO WAS AND EVER SHALL BE
Īśāno bhūta-bhavyasya

*The Person of the size of a thumb resides
within oneself; he is the Lord
of that which was and that which shall be.
One will never shrink away from him.
This, I now declare, is that!*

*The Person of the size of a thumb resides
within like a steady smokeless flame ñ
Lord of that which was and that which shall be,
the same both today and tomorrow.
This, I now declare, is that!*

LAST MANTRA

The *Ṛg-veda* is not the whole *śruti*, but it enunciates the most central part of it and lays the foundations for all the rest. It is befitting, then, to conclude this anthology with the final mantra of the *Ṛg-veda*, just as we opened it with the invocation of the first. Having traversed the long road of praise, exaltation, meditation, and sacrifice, having travelled through the upper realms of the Gods and the underworld of the demons, having reached the loftiest peaks of mystical speculation and touched the lowest depths of the human soul, having gazed, as far as we could, upon the cosmos and upon the divine, we arrive at this last stanza, which is dedicated to the human world and is a prayer for harmony and peace among Men by means of the protection of Agni and all the Gods, but ultimately through the acceptance by Men of their human calling. The last mantra knows only Man's ordinary language and Man's own cherished ideas; it comes back to the simplicity of the fact of being human: a union of hearts and a oneness of spirit, the overcoming of isolating individualisms by harmonious living together, because Man as person is always society and yet not plural. He is a unity with so many strings that they incur the risk of wars and strife, but also offer the possibility of a marvelous harmony and concord.

LAST MANTRA

samānī va ākūtiḥ
samānā hṛdayāni vaḥ
samānam astu vo mano
yathā vaḥ susahāsati

United your resolve, united your hearts,
may your spirits be at one,
that you may long together dwell
in unity and concord!